paines**PLOUGH**

TWENTY ONE
THEATRE ROYAL PLYMOUTH
years YEARS

hampstead theatre

THE STRAITS
by Gregory Burke

Cast *(in order of appearance)*

Darren	Calum Callaghan
Doink	James Marchant
Jock	Stephen Wight
Tracy	Jenny Platt

Director	John Tiffany
Designer	Neil Warmington
Lighting Designer	Natasha Chivers
Sound Designer	Cormac O'Connor
Movement	Steven Hoggett

Production Manager	Simon Sturgess
Company Stage Manager	Gary Morgan
Deputy Stage Manager	Alex Burke

Press Representative	Emma Schad
	07930 308018

Cover Image	Getty Images

First performed at the Traverse Theatre 1 August 2003

The playscript that follows was correct at time of going to press,
but may have changed during rehearsal.

THE COMPANY

Gregory Burke
Writer

Gregory Burke was born in Dunfermline in 1968. His first play Gagarin Way was produced by the Traverse Theatre in association with the National Theatre Studio in 2001, opening at the Edinburgh Fringe Festival then at the National Theatre and transferring to the Arts Theatre, West End in April 2002. The play won the Scotsman's First of the Firsts, Best New Play at the TMA Barclays Awards and shared the Meyer-Whitworth Award, it was nominated for a South Bank Theatre Award and the Laurence Olivier BBC Award for Best Play. Gregory was also awarded the Critics' Circle Most Promising Playwright in 2001. The play has since been translated into 17 different languages and produced all over the world. The Straits is his second play.

Calum Callaghan
Darren

Previous theatre work includes: Food Chain (Royal Court), Oliver (London Palladium), Les Miserables (Palace Theatre), Hey Mr Producer (Lyceum Theatre), Whistle Down the Wind (Sydmonton Festival/Aldwych Theatre). Television includes: Wall of Silence (Granada), The Bill (Freemantle), Stitch Up (BBC), I Am Rat (BBC), Writing and Pictures (BBC), Black Hearts in Battersea (BBC). Film work includes: Love, Honor and Obey (LH&O Ltd).

Natasha Chivers
Lighting Designer

For Paines Plough: The Drowned World, Helmet (also Traverse Theatre), Tiny Dynamite (also Frantic Assembly, Contact), Crazy Gary's Mobile Disco (also Sgript Cymru). Recent work includes: The Bomb-itty of Errors (New Ambassadors, London/Dublin), The Cherry Orchard (Oxford Stage Company), Playhouse Creatures (West Yorkshire Playhouse), Peepshow (Frantic Assembly, Plymouth Theatre Royal, Lyric Hammersmith), Wit (Stellar Quines, Tron, Traverse and Tour), After the Dance (Oxford Stage Company), Present Laughter (Bath Theatre Royal Productions), Among Unbroken Hearts (Traverse/Bush Theatre), A Chaste Maid In Cheapside (Almeida), 1001 Nights and The Firebird (Unicorn Theatre), Life with An Idiot (The Gate Theatre), A Listening Heaven (Royal Lyceum Theatre, Edinburgh), Eliza's House (Royal Exchange Theatre Manchester), Notre Dame De Paris (Strathcona Theatre Company/Lyric, Hammersmith), Hammerklavier (Theatre de Nesle, Paris) and Sweet Phoebe (Sydney Festival 2002).

Steven Hoggett
Movement

Steven is co-founder and Artistic Director with Frantic Assembly. Director / performer credits for Frantic include Look Back in Anger, Klub, Flesh, Zero, Sell Out, Hyms, Heavenly and Tiny Dynamite (co-production with Paines Plough). Directorial credits include Underworld and Peepshow for Frantic, Service Charge (Lyric Theatre, Hammersmith) and Air (MAC, Birmingham). Co-direction and choreography credits include Vs. (with Karim Tonsi Dance Company, Cairo), Waving (Oily Carte) and Improper (Bare Bones Dance Company). Additional performance credits include Manifesto (Volcano Theatre Company), Go Las Vegas (The Featherstonehaughs) and Outside Now for Prada (Milan Fashion Week 2001).

James Marchant
Doink

James trained at Drama Centre London, this is his first professional role. Previous work includes: Translations, The Seagull, All's Well that Ends Well, The Dutch Courtesan, The Strangeness of Others, A Month in the Country, Britannicus, Napoli Millionaria, This Happy Breed (Drama Centre London), William Poel Festival (Globe), Grange Hill (BBC TV) and various productions for Chicken Shed Theatre Company.

Cormac O'Connor
Sound Designer

Cormac has worked for a number of companies both in the British Isles and Internationally. His work includes Disco Pigs (Corcadorca), Laodmia (Merlin Theatre, Budapest) and The Oginski Polonaise (The Gate Biennelle).

Jenny Platt
Tracy

Jenny trained at East 15. Previous theatre work includes: Little Baby Nothing (Bush Theatre), Hanna and Hannah (UK Arts), Romeo and Juliet, Maid Marion (Whitehorse Theatre). Television work includes: The Bill (Freemantle).

John Tiffany
Director

John trained at Glasgow University and has been Associate Director at Paines Plough since 2001. Previously he was Literary Director at the Traverse. Theatre for Paines Plough includes: Helmet (Manchester Evening News Nomination for Best Production). Recent theatre includes Playhouse Creatures (West Yorkshire Playhouse), Falling (Bush Theatre). Theatre for the Traverse includes: Gagarin Way (also NT - First Of The Firsts, Herald Angel, Scotsman's Readers' Poll Awards and Olivier Award Nomination), Among Unbroken Hearts (also Bush Theatre), Abandonment, King Of The Fields, The Juju Girl, Danny 306 + Me (4 Ever) (also Birmingham Rep), Perfect Days (also Hampstead and Vaudeville - Fringe First Award and Oliver Award Nomination), Greta, Passing Places (also Citizens' and tour). Film includes: Karmic Mothers (BBC Tartan Shorts) and Golden Wedding (BBC Two Lives - MHM Award for Best Drama).

Under the Elms, Jane Eyre (Shared Experience), Don Juan, Love's Labours Lost, Ghosts, King Lear, Taming of the Shrew (English Touring Theatre), Dissent, Angels in America (7:84), Woyzeck, The Glass Menagerie, Comedians (Royal Lyceum, Edinburgh), Playhouse Creatures, Life is a Dream, Fiddler on the Roof (West Yorkshire Playhouse), The Duchess of Malfi (Bath Theatre Royal), Henry V (Royal Shakespeare Company), Much Ado About Nothing (Queen's, London), The Life of Stuff (Donmar Warehouse), Much Ado about Nothing, Waiting For Godot (Liverpool Everyman), The Tempest (Contact, Manchester), Women Laughing (Watford), Troilus & Cressida (Opera North), Oedipus Rex (Connecticut State Opera). His awards include: 3 TMA Awards for best design (Life is a Dream, Passing Places, Jane Eyre), The Linbury Prize for Stage Design, The Noel Machin memorial painting prize and The Sir Alfred Munnings Florence Prize for painting.

Neil Warmington
Designer

For Paines Plough: The Drowned World, Helmet (also Traverse Theatre), Splendour, Riddance, Crazyhorse. For Traverse Theatre: Gagarin Way, Wiping My Mothers Arse, Family, Passing Places, King of the Fields, Solemn Mass for a Full Moon in Summer (also Barbican Pit). Other work includes: Marriage of Figaro (Garsington Opera), Desire

Stephen Wight
Jock

Stephen trained at Drama Centre London. Previous theatre work includes: A Midsummer Nights Dream (RSC), Going Once (Musical Futures), As You Like It, Tartuffe, The Merchant of Venice, Anatol, Filumena (Drama Centre London). Television work includes: A Touch of Frost (ITV), Casualty (BBC).

TOUR DATES

1 - 23 August
Traverse Theatre, Edinburgh
Box Office 0131 228 1404
www.traverse.co.uk

5 - 6 September
Theatre Royal, Bury St Edmunds
Box Office 01284 769 505
www.theatreroyal.org

9 - 13 September
West Yorkshire Playhouse
Box Office 0113 213 7700
www.wyp.org.uk

14 - 25 October
The Drum, Theatre Royal Plymouth
Box Office 01752 267 222
www.theatreroyal.com

29 October - 29 November
Hampstead Theatre, London
Box Office 020 7722 9301
www.hampsteadtheatre.com

PAINES PLOUGH

"The legendary Paines Plough" Independent

The driving force behind Paines Plough is the vision of the playwright and the company has been discovering outstanding new voices in British theatre since 1974. We seek, encourage, develop, support and produce writers nation-wide, touring plays throughout the UK and Europe. At every level, writers are encouraged to be courageous in their work, to challenge our notions of theatre and the society we live in.

In 1997, Paines Plough appointed its sixth Artistic Director - Vicky Featherstone. Since Vicky's appointment, Paines Plough has gone from strength to strength making it one of the most vital theatre companies in Britain today.

Since 1997 Paines Plough has produced: THE DROWNED WORLD by Gary Owen, HELMET by Douglas Maxwell, TINY DYNAMITE by Abi Morgan, CRAZY GARY'S MOBILE DISCO by Gary Owen, SPLENDOUR by Abi Morgan, RIDDANCE by Linda McLean, THE COSMONAUT'S LAST MESSAGE TO THE WOMAN HE ONCE LOVED IN THE FORMER SOVIET UNION by David Greig, CRAVE by Sarah Kane, SLEEPING AROUND by Hilary Fannin, Stephen Greenhorn, Abi Morgan and Mark Ravenhill, CRAZYHORSE by Parv Bancil and THE WOLVES by Michael Punter.

This Other England
In 2001 Paines Plough was awarded the Peggy Ramsay Theatre Company of the Year for THIS OTHER ENGLAND, a cycle of plays which seeks to create an alternative census of the English language at the beginning of the 21st century.

The commissions are Simon Armitage, Biyi Bandele, David Greig, Linda McLean, Abi Morgan, Gary Owen, Philip Ridley, Peter Straughan and Enda Walsh.

The first of these commissions, PYRENEES by David Greig, will be produced in 2004.

International Work
Paines Plough is currently developing new projects and partnerships with Det Åpne Theatre in Oslo, the Royal Dramatic Theatre in Stockholm, Svenska Theatre in Helsinki and Aarhuus Theatre, Denmark. This work is funded by the British Council.

Wild Lunch
Wild Lunch is a regular Paines Plough festival of script-in-hand performances, born out of a selected writers group. The latest, Wild Lunch VII culminated in a sell-out season in June at the Young Vic.

PAINES PLOUGH

Artistic Director	Vicky Featherstone
Associate Director	John Tiffany
Managing Director	Tricia Mahoney
Literary Manager	Lucy Morrison
Adminstrator	Susannah Matthews
Associate Playwright	Glyn Cannon

PAINES PLOUGH BOARD OF DIRECTORS

Roanna Benn; Tamara Cizeika; Ian Codrington (Company Secretary); Giles Croft; David Edwards (Chair); Chris Elwell (Vice Chair); Fraser Grant; Clare O'Brien; Jenny Sealey

If you would like to be on Paines Plough's free mailing list, please send your details to:

Susannah Matthews
Paines Plough
4th Floor
43 Aldwych
LONDON WC2B 4DN

T + 44 (0) 20 7240 4533
F + 44 (0) 20 7240 4534
office@painesplough.com
www.painesplough.com

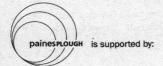 is supported by:

Paines Plough would like to thank Krista Madden for providing *Fake Bake* tans for Doink and Jock **www.beautyandthedirt.co.uk** and also Steve Warren for all his expert help with costumes.

DRUM THEATRE PLYMOUTH

The Drum Theatre Plymouth is a theatre of origination, serving Plymouth and the South-West. As a part of the Theatre Royal complex, it has become a leading force in the national development of writing, directing and producing relationships.

Recent premieres have included EDWARD GANT'S AMAZING FEATS OF LONELINESS by Anthony Nielson, THE GREEN MAN by Doug Lucie in a co-production with the Bush Theatre and MR PLACEBO by Isabel Wright in a collaboration with the Traverse Theatre.

In addition to THE STRAITS, our current autumn programme includes RABBIT by Brendan Cowell, fronted by our long time associates Frantic Assembly and Emma Frost's new play AIRSICK in co-operation with the Bush Theatre.

We also present the latest works from Graeae, Told by an Idiot, The Royal Court, The Red Room and Out of Joint.

Simon Stokes
Artistic Director

Drum Theatre, Royal Parade, Plymouth, PL1 2TR
01752 267 222
www.theatreroyal.com

HAMPSTEAD THEATRE

Hampstead Theatre moved into its RIBA award winning new building in February 2003 after over 40 years in a portacabin that was only expected to last for ten years.

Continuing Hampstead Theatre's policy of producing new plays by established writers and emerging writers, the opening season included plays by Stephen Adly Guirgis, Tanika Gupta and Tamsin Oglesby.

"Hampstead Theatre is on the crest of a wave" Sunday Times

THE STRAITS by Gregory Burke is part of Anthony Clark's first season as Artistic Director. The season also includes plays from established writers Clare McIntyre, Stephen Lowe and Hanif Kureishi; a first play from a young Canadian poet, Drew Pautz and an original play by Barbara Norden for 7 – 11 year olds.

THE MATH'S TUTOR by Clare McIntyre	25.09.03 - 25.10.03
THE STRAITS by Gregory Burke	29.10.03 - 29.11.03
METEORITE by Barbara Norden	04.12.03 - 03.01.04
REVELATIONS by Stephen Lowe	10.12.03 - 31.01.04
ALL THIS STUFF by Drew Pautz	05.02.04 - 06.03.04
WHEN THE NIGHT BEGINS by Hanif Kureishi	11.03.04 - 17.04.04

Anthony Clark
Artistic Director

James Williams
Executive Director

hampstead theatre

Hampstead Theatre, Eton Avenue, Swiss Cottage, London, NW3 3EU
020 7722 9301
www.hampsteadtheatre.com

A CHRONOLOGY OF THE FALKLANDS WAR

1982

2 April	Argentine Forces occupy the Falkland Islands.
12 April	Britain declares maritime exclusion zone two hundred miles around the Falklands.
1 May	First British attacks on the Falklands Islands.
2 May	Argentine cruiser General Belgrano sunk.
4 May	HMS Sheffield hit by exocet missile.
21 May	British Forces establish beachhead on Falklands Islands. HMS Ardent sunk. Fifteen Argentine planes shot down.
23 May	HMS Antelope sunk.
25 May	HMS Coventry sunk.
28 May	British victory at battle of Goose Green.
4 June	Britain and USA veto UN call for an immediate ceasefire.
11-14 June	British Forces close on Port Stanley.
14 June	Argentine Forces surrender.
17 June	General Galtieri resigns as head of Argentine ruling military junta.

1983

9 June	Margaret Thatcher re-elected as Prime Minister of Britain.

Gregory Burke
The Straits

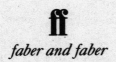

faber and faber

First published in 2003
by Faber and Faber Limited
3 Queen Square London WC1N 3AU
Published in the United States by Faber and Faber Inc.
an affiliate of Farrar, Straus and Giroux LLC, New York

Typeset by Country Setting, Kingsdown, Kent CT14 8ES
Printed in England by Mackays of Chatham plc, Chatham, Kent

A CIP record for this book
is available from the British Library

ISBN 0-571-22158-0

2 4 6 8 10 9 7 5 3 1

To Val

Acknowledgements

I would like to thank

BBC Scotland Radio Drama Department

Alan Brodie and everyone at ABR

Everyone at Paines Plough

Special thanks to Vicky Featherstone
and John Tiffany for all their help and support

Characters

Doink
Jock
Darren
Tracy

SCENE ONE

Gibraltar. 2 May 1982.

Rosia Bay. A mole beside the sea. A low wall. The area surrounding the wall is dirty and run-down, dotted with detritus from the sea. Two teenage boys are onstage. Both are wearing swimming trunks. Doink (sixteen), dark-haired, tanned and athletic, is crouching on the wall looking out to sea, cradling a speargun in his arms like a rifle. Darren (fifteen), blond-haired, a recent arrival in Gibraltar, lacks the tan and physique that comes from living an outdoor life. He sits on the wall wrapped in a towel. Beside the wall lie two large diver's bags around which are scattered the equiment of a snorkelling expedition – flippers, masks, wetsuits.

Doink They brought him in here after.

Darren Yeah?

Doink Yeah.

Pause.

His body. He was dead.

Darren Yeah?

Doink Yeah.

Pause.

Darren I've been on the *Victory*. Back in Pompey. Went with the school.

Doink They patched it up in here. Before it went home. It was in a shit state after Trafalgar. (*Points out over the sea.*) It's just over there. Trafalgar.

Pause.

Fuckin amazin.

Darren Yeah?

Doink History innit. (*Doink stands up, shifting the speargun to his shoulder.*) They had him in a barrel of brandy. Stops you goin off. Brandy. They put the barrel up in Peppertree Cottage. (*Doink turns to Darren and points upwards.*) Up there. Then they took him back to England an buried him. (*Doink jumps down from the wall.*) You don't know her, but there's this bird comes down here. Sharon. Blonde hair. Not bad. Her dad reckons he saw him.

Darren Who?

Doink Nelson.

Darren Straight.

Doink He was workin up there or somethin an he was in the cottage an some bloke's standin an he says, alright mate? But the bloke don't answer. Then he thinks, hang on, what's this bloke in fancy dress for, cos he's in the old uniform with the one arm an the hat an that . . .

Darren He wouldn't be in his uniform.

Doink You what?

Darren If he's in a barrel of brandy he wouldn't be in his uniform.

Doink No, he's in Peppertree Cottage.

Darren Yeah. But if he's in the barrel when he was up there.

Doink He ain't in the fuckin barrel. He's standin in the fuckin room.

Darren They'd strip him before they put him in the barrel. Then if he come out he'd be bollock-naked.

Doink He's a ghost. He ain't gonna go around bollock-naked if he's a ghost is he? You don't get bollock-naked ghosts.

Pause.

I'm only telling you what she told me. (*Doink climbs back onto the wall.*)

Darren Dunno if I believe in all that ghosts an stuff.

Doink Full of ghosts, Gib. All these old houses an graves an that. All the fightin there's been. You've only been here a coupla weeks, you ain't had the chance to see nothin. Even under the Rock, yeah, there's a whole like town in there all waitin for if there's a war. There's like roads an villages an stuff an hospitals and stores an everythin. It's all there, ready. (*Doink's attention is caught by something in the water. He concentrates on the point, aiming the gun.*) Here he comes.

Darren joins him.

(*Points.*) Over there. At the boom. We'll find out what's happenin now. Jock, he always gets somethin. He's got occy eyes. Sees them every time he does. Don't matter what they do or where they hide or how deep they are. I've been fuckin tellin him somethin's happenin. We ain't caught nothin for a couple of weeks. If he ain't got somethin today then we'll know the spics are at it.

Pause.

Darren Are no Gibraltarians allowed in here?

Doink Spics, mate. No fuckin way. The spics all stay round at Camp Bay. Rosia's for us. British only. The spics might say they're British but they're only fuckin British cos this place belongs to us. It's us that puts the food in their fuckin mouths. They might all be called Albert an fuckin George an Montgomery an stuff but they're all fuckin spics when it comes to it. You'll find out at school on Monday. Anti-English day.

Darren Yeah. I heard about that.

Doink They better stay out of here an all if they know what's fuckin good for them. (*He jumps down from the wall and goes to his bag. He puts down the speargun and pulls a large diving knife and a sharpener from the bag.*) He must have gone round Seven Sisters. (*sharpening the knife*) We got an occy round there last summer. It was a mad one. I shot it. It went in this pipe to get away. My spear's stickin in it so I dives down to try an pull it out an it shoots back out the pipe with this bleedin great conger eel munchin away on the other end of it. Fuckin shat myself I did. I was like pullin the occy out the pipe an the conger's pullin it in. Jock dives down beside me and shoots his gun in the pipe. The conger lets go an I pulls it out. Fuckin massive it was. Honestly, mate. I was standin like this – (*He holds his arm straight out from his shoulder.*) – an its tentacles were trailin on the ground. We got twenty quid for it off the moggy in the restaurant in Camp Bay. We was fuckin smashed that night. (*Laughs.*) Jock ended up havin to get his stomach pumped.

Darren Twenty quid.

Doink If we'd taken it down to the fish market in town we'd have got thirty quid at least. Moggy bastard. If we were spics they'd have given us more. You've gotta watch with Moroccans. Rob you fuckin blind.

Pause.

Fuck you too, if they get the chance.

Darren Yeah?

Doink Specially if you've got blond hair.

Darren Yeah?

Doink Oh yeah. They love blond hair.

> *Jock (sixteen) enters. Like Doink, he is tanned and athletic. He is wearing the top half of a wetsuit, swimming trunks and flippers. He is carrying a speargun in one hand and the spear from the gun in the other. There is a small octopus on the end of the spear.*

Where have you fuckin been?

Jock (*drops the gun, spear and octopus and pulls off his mask and snorkel*) Fuckin freezin. (*He picks up a towel and begins vigorously drying his legs.*)

Doink Where d'you go?

Jock I knew I should have put on the whole suit. (*He starts rubbing his crotch.*) Won't see me bollocks for a week.

Doink Your balls ain't dropped yet. (*Doink drops the knife and picks up the spear with the octopus on the end of it.*)

Doink (*to Jock*) Is that it?

Jock (*nods*) D'you see anythin?

> *Doink shakes his head.*

(*Jock removes his wetsuit jacket and continues drying himself.*) A lot of oil in the water today.

Doink There's always a lot of oil in the water.

Jock Yeah, but, it's fuckin thick. Specially with all the ships goin in and out. (*to Darren*) D'you see anythin?

Darren I didn't last very long.

Jock Yeah, it's warm out here, but you need a wetsuit in the water.

Doink unscrews the end of the spear. The point comes off in his hand. He pulls the spear from the octopus.

Doink (*to Jock*) Where d'you get it?

Jock The other side of the rocks.

Doink I was over there.

Jock (*picks up the speargun and begins to screw the point back on it*) I nearly missed it. But it moved onto the sand. Didn't have nowhere to hide then. (*to Darren*) They ain't fast, occies. They have to try an blend in. Change colour. Stay still, yeah. Try and look like what surrounds them.

Doink They're sneaky fuckers.

Jock They let you miss them. But they're there. (*He puts the spear back in the gun.*) Once you see them it's easy. You just dive down . . . nice and slow. (*He tracks the imaginary target and stops when he has Darren in his sights. He mimes pulling the trigger.*) You just gotta know what you're lookin for.

Jock and Doink look at one another. Doink picks up the knife.

Doink Come here Daz.

Darren stands up and goes over to Doink reluctantly.

(*Turns the octopus over.*) See the beak there?

Darren (*looking at the octopus warily*) Yeah.

Doink The bite they give you with that. It'll go right through a wetsuit. Show him your arm, Jock.

Jock holds out his arm.

14

It was a much bigger one than this. Still gotta be careful with the little ones though. (*He moves closer to Darren.*) To finish them, yeah, before you sell them.

Darren Yeah.

Doink You've got to turn their heads inside out. (*Holds out the knife to Darren.*) Take that. (*Holds up the octopus.*) See, their heads are like hoods, yeah. You put your hand up the back off the hood. (*He does it.*) Turn it inside out. (*He turns the hood of the octopus inside out.*) Like that, yeah. (*to Darren*) That's the brains there, yeah, on either side. You gotta cut them off.

　Pause.

Come on.

　Darren hands the knife to Doink.

Darren You show me.

　Doink takes the knife.

Doink You put the knife through there – (*He puts the knife blade between the octopus brain and the hood.*) – like that, yeah, the brains attached at each end, you slice through – (*He slices from side to side.*) – an off it comes. (*The octopus drops to the ground.*) There you go, one half of an occy's brain. Which you – (*He throws it away.*) – chuck. (*to Darren*) Go on. Take the knife.

　Darren takes the knife from Doink and picks up the octopus.

Slide it in there, between the brain an the head.

Darren Like that?

Doink Now cut it off.

　Darren starts cutting.

Cut it.

Darren I am cuttin it.

Doink Harder. Like you're sawin.

Darren saws his way through the brain until it comes away in his hand. He rolls it between his fingers.

Darren They don't half feel funny. (*Points to something on the occy.*) What's that?

Doink That's the ink sac. Give us the knife.

Doink takes the knife from Darren and cuts the ink sac from the octopus. He gives it to Darren.

That's what they spray at you.

Doink says something to Darren, who looks at Jock. Doink nods. Darren hesitates. Doink nods again. Darren throws the ink sac at Jock. It bursts when it hits him, covering him in ink.

Jock Oi.

Jock jumps up and chases Darren and Doink onto the wall. Doink keeps Jock at bay with the octopus and the knife.

Doink (*laughing*) It's only a little ink, mate.

Jock (*looking at the ink on him*) I'm gonna have to go back in the water now.

Pause.

Wankers.

Jock exits to go back into the sea. Doink and Darren come down from the wall. Doink drops the octopus on the ground near his diver's bag.

Darren How come he's called Jock?

Doink He's from Scotland. That's where they come from. Jocks.

Darren He don't sound like a Jock.

Doink He ain't lived there for years. Lived all over he has. Pompey. Plymouth. He's been out here for ever.

Darren Is he alright?

Doink Alfuckinright?

Pause.

He's the fuckin best, mate.

Pause.

Darren What d'you reckon we'll get?

Doink What?

Darren For the occy? What d'you reckon? A fiver?

Doink We'll never get a fiver for that. Get fuckin laughed at. It ain't even the length of your arm. Waste of time goin all the way down the fish market.

Darren What about one of the restaurants. The moggy?

Doink He don't work round there any more.

Jock re-enters and begins drying himself again.

They don't buy nothin now. Not unless you're a fuckin spic. (*Picks up his speargun and begins to examine the rubber band which fires the spear.*) Dunno how the fuck I'm supposed to catch anythin with this piece of shit. (*Doink removes the spear from the gun and looks down its length.*) I think the spear's bent from when I hit that rock last week. (*Shows the spear to Jock.*) Look.

Jock takes the spear and peers down its length.

Doink It's bent innit?

Jock It's alright.

Doink It's bent.

Jock You're fuckin bent.

Doink You'd fuckin know. (*Examines the spear. To Darren*) Told me mum to get me a new one for the summer. A nice compressed-air one.

Jock Spoiled you are.

Doink No I ain't.

Jock You fuckin are, mate.

> *Doink picks up a flipper which is lying near him and throws it at Jock, who dodges it. Jock removes a T-shirt from his bag and puts it on.*

Doink Don't matter what she buys me if there's fuck all to catch. (*to Jock*) We should come down here more an keep an eye on the place. Make sure no fuckin spics are at it. Member the last time? That spic who come down here?

Jock It was only one bloke.

Doink (*to Darren*) He was older than us. He was the same age as my brother. He was comin down here at night. They feed at night, occies. Fucker had an aqualung. He killed loads, even the fuckin baby ones. (*to Jock*) If you've got a fuckin aqualung it ain't fair, is it? (*to Darren*) We jumped him.

Jock We never fuckin jumped him.

Doink We did.

Jock Steve and – (*to Darren*) – his brother. And the older lads jumped him.

Doink We was fuckin there.

Jock We didn't do nothin.

Doink We was still fuckin there.

Pause.

Darren (*to Doink*) Wish I had a brother.

Doink (*to Darren*) He's in the Navy now.

Darren Yeah?

Doink He's in the Falklands. On the *Sheffield*.

Jock and Doink begin to gather their kit and pack it away in their bags and begin to dress in shorts, T-shirts and trainers.

Darren You reckon there's gonna be a war?

Doink Too fuckin right, mate.

Jock Whatever happens, the sooner they get the border back open the better. Fuckin World Cup's startin in fuckin two months, a couple of miles away, an they fuckin shut the border.

Doink Fuckin spic bastards.

Jock Scotland's playin in Malaga. We could be fuckin there in an hour.

Doink Who wants to go an watch that shit?

Pause.

Darren My dad reckons the Argies'll give up, now we've scraped together enough ships to go down there. Reckons they'll sail round the islands a few times and they'll shit themselves and surrender.

Doink They wouldn't send them all the way down there for nothin, would they? If we let the Argies have the Falklands the Spanish could just walk in here an have this place.

Pause.

Darren Saw them doin up that hospital ship in the dockyard. They were workin on it all night.

Doink They'll only need it for the fuckin Argies once the Marines get down there. (*to Darren*) I'm joinin the Marines.

Darren Yeah?

Doink Both of us are. Ain't we, Jock?

Jock nods.

Fuckin right, mate. Get a green beret.

Darren Yeah.

Doink Me old boy says there's only three choices in life if you're from Pompey or Plymouth. Work in the dockyard, join the Navy or join the Marines. My old man works in the yard, my brother's in the Navy, I'll join the Marines.

Jock Full house.

Doink Completes the set.

Darren When you goin in them?

Doink After summer. Gotta wait for the new intake.

Darren So you'll be leavin?

Doink Yeah.

Pause.

But this place'll still be here. And it'll need lookin after. (*Doink puts his pack on his back. He picks up his speargun and cradles it in his arms. To Darren*) You comin for a yomp?

Darren A yomp?

Doink A fuckin run.

Jock Straight up the hill to BV.

Jock puts his bag on his back. Tracy (sixteen), blonde, very pretty, enters.

Darren What you doin here?

Tracy Oh that's nice. What happened to hello, sis?

Darren What d'you want?

Tracy Get you home.

Doink He's comin for a run.

Pause.

Tracy *(to Doink)* Are you talkin to me?

Pause.

Doink Yeah.

Tracy Well, don't.

Pause.

(to Darren) Come on.

Pause.

Darren. *(Tracy exits.)*

Darren I better go.

Doink Ain't you comin with us?

Darren No . . . I . . . *(Holds up the octopus. To Jock)* Can I keep this?

Jock Eh . . . yeah.

Darren looks around and finds an old plastic bag. He puts the octopus in it.

Doink We'll call on you tomorrow.

Darren Yeah. See you. (*Darren exits.*)

Doink What was her problem?

Jock I dunno.

   Pause.

Doink You might have said somethin.

Jock What?

Doink I dunno. Somethin.

   Pause.

Jock She was fuckin lovely.

SCENE TWO

Darren sits in the living room of a typical 'married quarters' house, watching a violent war film on video. He has the plastic bag at his feet. Tracy enters. She sits down. They watch the television.

Darren They're my mates.

Tracy What?

Darren They're my mates.

Tracy You're welcome to them.

   They sit in silence. We hear the noise of machine-gun fire and screams coming from the television.

Are you sure they're your mates?

   Darren concentrates on the television.

Tracy Just watch yourself is all I'm sayin.

Darren Shut up, will you?

Tracy You know what's happened before when you think people are your mates . . .

Darren They're alright.

Tracy Are you sure?

    Pause.

Darren (*picks up the remote control*) Let me show you this bit.

Tracy You're alright.

Darren No, I'll show you.

Tracy I don't want to see it.

Darren He stitches his own arm up.

Tracy What?

Darren He's got a compass and . . .

Tracy How can he stitch his arm with a compass?

Darren No. Rambo, he's got all this stuff in the handle of his knife. A compass an like a needle an thread an stuff. When he cuts his arm he stitches it up with the needle an thread. It's brilliant.

Tracy Watchin soldiers an playin soldiers. Is that all you an your mates can do?

Darren They ain't playin soldiers.

Tracy It looks like it.

Darren They ain't playin.

Tracy How old are they? Ten?

Darren Sixteen.

    Pause.

Same age as you.

Tracy I'm seventeen.

Darren Just.

    Pause.

They're in trainin. Doink's goin in the Marines. You gotta be fit to go in the Marines.

Tracy Fuckin Action Man more like.

Darren They're yompin.

Tracy Yompin?

Darren Yeah. Like when you go runnin with all your kit. Long-distance runnin. In the Marines, yeah, they call it yompin.

    Pause.

Tracy You wouldn't think they'd get sunstroke, not after bein out here so long.

Darren They're in trainin.

Tracy It's fuckin sunstroke, bruv.

    Pause.

What do they have in them packs anyway?

Darren Snorkellin stuff. Wetsuits.

    Pause.

Weightbelts. For weight.

    Pause.

Bricks.

Tracy Bricks? They gonna be commando bricklayers are they? They parachute in when someone needs a wall put up.

Darren I'm gonna get myself a pack, start goin trainin with them.

Tracy And why would you want to do that?

Darren Get fit an that. Go spearfishin an stuff.

Tracy Be like them.

Darren Maybe.

> *Pause.*

I might even think about joinin up or somethin.

Tracy You couldn't handle that.

Darren Who says?

Tracy There is no way you're throwin your life away in the Army.

> *Darren goes into the bag at his feet and pulls out the dismembered octopus that was caught earlier.*

Darren.

Darren What?

Tracy What you doin with that?

Darren I brought it home.

Tracy You can't keep that in here.

Darren How?

Tracy It's fuckin disgustin.

Darren (*stroking the octopus*) They're alright.

> *Pause.*

You know how you kill them?

Tracy I don't. Funny that, innit?

Darren You turn their head inside out an cut their brains off.

Tracy Shut up.

Darren You do. (*He points to either side of the hood.*) They've got two brains.

Tracy Well, that's two more than you an your fuckin mates then.

> *Pause.*

Darren Where d'you go last night?

Tracy Never you mind.

Darren I won't say nothin.

> *Pause.*

Tracy Just went to the pub.

Darren Which pub?

Tracy The one down at the barracks.

Darren Oh yeah.

Tracy No.

> *Pause.*

It was packed in there last night.

Darren Who d'you go there with?

Tracy Never you mind.

> *Pause.*

Darren Doink's brother's in the Navy.

Tracy Is he?

Darren He's in the Falklands.

Tracy Is he.

Darren Yeah.

Pause.

Where is the Falklands?

Tracy laughs.

I know it's near the Argies somewhere . . .

Tracy It's in the South Atlantic.

Pause.

A little spot in the middle of nowhere. Dunno why they're havin a war over it.

Darren There must be somethin. They wouldn't send them all the way down there for nothin.

Pause.

Tracy All the blokes in the pub last night. They were all usin it to try an get your knickers off.

Darren That ain't hard.

Tracy What?

Darren Nothin.

Tracy They were all sayin, it's gonna be us that's goin next. All usin the same line. Our unit's goin next, we've been told we're on forty-eight hours' notice. I said to them, you must think I'm fuckin soft, mate, if you think I'm gonna fall for that shit.

Darren You fell for it before.

Tracy I never fell for nothin.

Darren That's how you're in so much shit. (*Laughs.*) Gettin caught with a sailor.

Tracy I never got caught with a sailor.

Darren You did.

Tracy I got caught in the Buccaneer. It's a club.

Pause.

Darren With a sailor.

Pause.

Tracy Yeah.

Pause.

I wasn't doin nothin.

Darren You're always goin on about how you ain't ever gonna go with no sailors, you're doin A Levels an you're gonna be this an that an you come out here for two weeks and get caught doin that.

Pause.

Tracy It's Mum that went mental. No one else's mum goes mental.

Darren You know what she's like.

Tracy She overreacts to everythin.

Pause.

I dunno what her problem is. Dad was a sailor when she met him.

Pause.

Darren You know how you ain't allowed out.

Tracy I am allowed out.

Darren No you ain't.

Tracy I am.

Darren School and work. That's the only time you get to leave the house.

Tracy Shut up.

Pause.

Darren You workin tomorrow?

Tracy No.

Pause.

Darren At your work, yeah?

Tracy I ain't workin.

Darren No, I mean, at your work, yeah, do they do like, you know cook, serve octopus?

Tracy Yeah.

Darren Where do they get them?

Tracy I dunno.

Darren They buy them at the fish market?

Tracy I dunno. I'm a waitress. I ain't the fuckin chef.

Pause.

Darren You get a pound a pound at some restaurants, Doink says. They can make twenty quid for a big one. I know we only got this today but that's cos Doink reckons that the spics are comin in at night an nickin them.

Pause.

They hate us, the spics.

Tracy I wonder why.

Darren They used to buy octopus off the lads where you work till the spics come along.

Tracy No one's gonna buy that.

Darren I ain't talkin about this one. I . . .

Pause.

It wouldn't hurt to ask.

Tracy No.

Darren You went out last night when Mum and Dad were out an I didn't say nothin.

Tracy Cos I'd kill you.

Darren Still didn't say nothin.

Pause.

Tracy You ain't bribin me . . .

Darren I don't wanna bribe you. I just want you to ask.

Pause.

Tracy What's in it for me?

Darren You can go out. I'll tell Mum you're with me.

Tracy Yeah, right.

Darren I will.

Pause.

Tracy She'll know somethin's up.

Darren No she won't.

Tracy She will. When do I ever go anywhere with you?

Darren She trusts me.

Pause.

Tomorrow, yeah. Leave the house with me then go round your work an ask, come down to Rosia an tell us what they say an then you can go an do what you want after that. I'll say you were with me. All day.

Pause.

Come on. Please.

Pause.

I'll help you whenever you wanna go out.

Pause.

Tracy (*points at the octopus*) If I do. And I haven't said I will. I ain't takin that with me. It fuckin stinks worse than you.

SCENE THREE

3 May 1982. Rosia Bay.
    Doink, Jock and Darren are preparing to go spearfishing. Their kit is spread around them as before. Doink and Jock are putting on their wetsuits.

Doink Fuckin *General* fuckin *Belgrano*. Wankers. (*to Darren*) I told you, mate, we was gonna go down there and kick the shit out of them fuckin Argy bastards.

Jock Stupid fuckin name for a boat anyway.

Darren It was a sub that got it.

Doink Fuckin teach them to go in the fuckin exclusion zone. Silly spic bastards don't listen when they're warned. They get zapped. Bet Steve and all his mates were chuffed. They'd all be havin a party on the old shiny *Sheffield*. I was writin to him this mornin sayin I bet you're chuffed.

Jock It weren't the Sheffield.

Doink Yeah, they'd all be celebratin an that.

31

Pause.

Darren (*to Doink*) What does Steve do?

Doink Radar.

Darren Radar?

Doink Yeah.

Jock That ain't proper fightin is it? That's not war. Sittin watchin what's goin on on a screen. It's like playin fuckin space invaders.

Doink What you fuckin sayin?

Jock When you just sit there lookin at a screen.

Doink Yeah, well, at least he's there. That's why I wanna go in the Marines. I wanna be in combat. Proper combat.

Pause.

Jock What d'you reckon it's like to kill someone?

Darren It must be weird, yeah.

Doink They reckon it's more difficult than it looks.

Darren Yeah?

Doink Yeah. It takes a lot to kill people. Unless you shoot them in the head or the heart or somethin. But if you're stabbin someone or like beatin them to death you've gotta really fuckin try.

Darren How come Bruce Lee can do that one-inch punch stuff then when he just taps you on the head an like half an hour later you're dead?

Doink That's a lot of bollocks is what that is.

Darren No it ain't. I've seen it on video.

Pause.

Doink Reckon my grandad must have killed a few.

Jock Mine too.

Doink You think of all that went on in the old days
an that it stands to reason that they've killed someone.
I always remember my grandad with his medals an that.
All laid out on St George's Day when he would go down
the Legion.

Jock North Africa. That's where mine was. Desert Rat,
he was. He got shot in the face once.

Darren Jokin?

Jock Well, not shot. It was shrapnel from a shell. He
was a despatch rider an he was ridin his motorbike, yeah,
this shell hits the road right in front of him, an his bike
an him go straight in the fuckin hole. He's lyin in the hole
an his bike's fucked an he's broke his arm an a couple of
ribs an he says he can feel all his teeth are smashed and
his mouth's full of blood. The shrapnel went in one cheek
an out the other. Took all his teeth out. He's lying there
an all of a sudden this big German jumps in beside him
and my grandad's thinkin, fuck it I'm a goner, an then
the German fuckin shrugs an helps him up an gets out
a smoke and gives one to my grandad an they sit there
havin a smoke an a chat an that. Cept he said he couldn't
talk or smoke because he had this big fuckin hole in his
face. The German finishes his fag an goes. So my grandad
he sits there an he thinks he better get a move on or he's
gonna bleed to death. He climbs out the hole an legs it till
he finds some British an they take him to hospital. The
hospital stitched his face up but it made him look like he
was smiling all the time cos they just pulled his cheeks
back and stitched them together. An they gave him this
massive set of falsers, yeah. So he looked like he was
really happy all the time. He worked in a butcher's after
that. No one knew a fuckin word he was sayin.

Doink Done his bit though.

Jock Yeah.

Doink Everyone in my family's done their bit.

Jock Same here.

Darren And me.

Doink It goes all the way back, don't it? England an fightin an that. War's what we do innit. What we do best. Don't matter who we fight either. Spics or Germans or French or whatever. Reckon we'll always be at war with someone and we always win.

Pause.

Darren Do you reckon the Argies'll give up now?

Doink This is just the start, mate. That's their navy fucked. Do their army now. (*Doink rummages in his bag and comes out with a wetsuit jacket. To Darren*) I brought this for you.

Darren Cheers.

Doink It's an old one of Steve's.

Darren starts putting on the jacket.

It might be a bit too big. But you'll need it if we're gonna have a good look around. See what the spics have been up to. (*He rummages in the bag again. He pulls out a huge diving knife.*)

Darren Bloody hell.

Doink (*pulls it from the sheath and cuts the air*) This is Steve's an all. All his stuff's still in the house for when he comes on holiday. (*to Jock*) Reckon I might take this into school tomorrow.

Jock You'll need it.

Doink You shittin it already, are you?

Jock There's gonna be hundreds of them, all over from the estates and that.

Doink Honestly, Daz, you'll love it.

Darren (*unenthusiastic and struggling with the wetsuit trousers*) Yeah. Can't wait.

Jock It ain't just gonna be kids from school.

Darren (*to Doink*) Yeah?

Doink (*to Jock*) Yeah. But it's the one time all the British kids join up an all. Europa an the Foreshore lot an North Camp.

Jock There still ain't enough of us.

Doink Don't matter how many there are long as we all stand and fight.

   Pause.

You're alright anyway, Jock. All your mates'll look after you. (*to Darren*) He's the only English kid to play for a spic team.

Darren How come, Jock?

Jock Cos they're good. Navy Colts and RAF are fuckin rubbish. And Tower? Fuck me. We beat them fifty-six–nothin last season. I scored nine. And I'm the right back.

   They all laugh.

Darren Who d'you play for, Doink?

   Jock laughs.

Doink Navy Colts.

Jock laughs again.

(*to Jock*) At least I ain't a fuckin traitor. We'll be keepin our eye on you, won't we, Darren? No room for anyone lettin their mates down tomorrow?

> *Darren stands up in the trousers which he can't quite get on.*

Darren This is a bit tight.

Jock You want it tight.

Darren I'm gettin pins and needles. (*He stretches inside the jacket.*) So what happens then? Tomorrow. Anti-English day.

Jock We all get our heads kicked in.

Doink No we don't. They have it every year, mate.

Darren Why?

Doink They just do. It's always happened.

> *Pause.*

This is our last one this year. (*to Darren*) I remember my first one. I was shittin it. But once you've done it, piece of piss.

Jock I hate it.

Doink Next year you'll be tellin all the new lads how easy it is.

> *Pause.*

Darren My sister was sayin they don't have one at the girls' comp.

Jock (*to Darren*) So what's your sister like, then?

Darren She's alright.

Doink She didn't seem very happy yesterday.

Darren She's in trouble with me mum. She ain't allowed out.

Jock What she do?

Darren I can't really say, mate.

Doink You can tell us.

Pause.

Darren You won't tell her I said?

Doink No way.

Darren I dunno exactly what happened. No one tells me nothin. But I think she was out in town and she got caught with some sailor or somethin.

Pause.

Jock And . . .

Darren That's it.

Jock That's it.

Doink That's fuck all, mate. You should hear about his sister.

Jock She's a fuckin slag, mate.

Darren Yeah?

Jock She's back home now. But she used to drive me mum and dad mad.

Doink (*laughing*) Member that time the Redcaps found her in the barracks with all them squaddies.

Jock My old boy went mental. He said it's bad enough you've had half the Navy, but, fuck me, the Army.

Doink Yeah. She used to do alright for a dog.

Jock (*laughing*) Yeah.

Darren I don't think my sister's as bad as that.

Jock She ain't a dog anyway.

Darren I think me mum went mad cos she doesn't want her fuckin up her exams.

Doink Exams?

Darren She's stayin on to do her A Levels.

Jock A Levels?

Darren Yeah.

Jock Fuckin hell.

Doink Fuckin A Levels.

Pause.

Jock What's she gonna be?

Darren Dunno.

Doink She must be gonna be somethin if she's doin A Levels.

Darren She's really good at school an that.

Jock You wouldn't think it. To look at her.

Doink We better get a fuckin shift on. (*to Darren*) How's that jacket?

Darren (*does up the zip of the wetsuit jacket*) It's a bit nippy under the arms.

Doink (*tries stretching the jacket a bit*) It's fine.

Jock (*goes over to Darren*) And I brought you this. (*He hands Darren a fearsome-looking gaff.*)

Darren looks at it uncertainly. Jock takes the gaff back from Darren and wields it demonstratively before handing it back to Darren.

Jock It's rusty. But it'll do the job.

Darren Cheers.

Doink You're beginning to look the part now. (*to Jock*) Get a move on, mate.

Tracy enters carrying a bag. She is wearing a very short dress and a pair of trainers.

Jock (*to Tracy*) Alright?

Tracy ignores Jock.

Darren Alright?

Tracy Yeah.

Darren You took your time.

Tracy (*looks Darren up and down and laughs*) What d'you fuckin look like?

Doink He looks alright.

Pause.

Tracy (*she turns to Doink*) You're Dink?

Doink Doink.

Tracy That's it. (*Indicates Darren.*) He went on and on about you at home. Hardly shut up about how good you are at cutting up little animals with big knives. I think he's got a little bit of a crush.

Darren What did he say?

Tracy Who?

Darren The bloke at your work. Who d'you think? (*to Doink*) She works at the –

Tracy Who's she?

Darren – she works at the restaurant round at Camp Bay.

Doink Yeah?

Darren I asked her to find out whether we could sell occies round there.

Doink (*to Tracy*) What d'he say?

Tracy He said, yeah. Whatever you catch you can take it round there. Just make sure it's a decent size. (*to Doink*) Nothin too small.

> *Pause.*

Doink We better go an get some then. (*to Darren*) Well done, Daz. (*to Jock*) Looks like it's gonna be a good summer.

> *Darren smiles. Tracy kicks off her trainers.*

Darren What you doin?

Tracy What d'you think I'm doin.

Darren Don't you want to get off somewhere?

Tracy No.

Darren I thought you were gonna go off somewhere.

Tracy I'm gonna have a swim. It's hot, innit? Or ain't you noticed?

Doink This ain't hot.

Tracy What d'you say, lover?

Doink I said this ain't hot.

> *Pause.*

Not like real summer's hot.

Tracy Well, I'm pretty hot. (*She takes her dress off. She is wearing a bikini. To Doink*) I'm allowed, ain't I?

Jock Yeah. Go ahead.

Tracy Or is this a boys-only bit of sea?

Pause.

Doink It's a free country.

Tracy Good.

Jock It's cold in there.

Tracy Yeah. I'll have a bit of a sunbathe then. Got to start gettin a tan.

Tracy takes a towel from her bag, lays it on the ground and lies on it to sunbathe.

Doink (*stands up. To Jock and Darren*) Let's go.

Darren gets up. Jock does not move.

Let's go.

Jock does not move.

Jock.

Jock stays sitting.

What's wrong with you?

Jock Nothin.

Doink Let's go then.

Jock I dunno if I can be bothered.

Doink You what?

Pause.

Come on.

Jock No.

Doink No?

Jock I ain't goin.

Doink Why?

Jock I only just had somethin to eat, mate. You gotta wait. Don't wanna get cramp.

Doink Fuckin cramp.

Jock I'm stayin here. (*Jock pulls his towel towards him and places it on his lap.*) For a bit.

   Doink looks at Jock, exasperated.

Doink Well I'm off.

Tracy (*to Doink*) Pass me me suntan oil, someone.

   Doink picks up her bag and throws it to her.

Darren Where d'you wanna head for, Doink?

Tracy I've heard some stupid names before –

Darren It ain't stupid.

Jock (*to Tracy*) Yeah, I always thought it was a stupid name.

Doink (*moves towards Jock*) You what?

   Jock jumps up and away from Doink. Still with the towel. He adjusts himself.

Doink I'll give you a slap.

Jock Sorry, mate.

   Pause.

But it is a bit . . .

   Darren picks up Jock's speargun.

Darren (*to Jock*) Come on, mate. I ain't gonna be able to see them. You gotta show me how it's done.

Jock You'll be alright.

Darren I won't.

Jock thinks. Jock picks up his flippers, mask and snorkel.

Jock (*to Darren*) Come on then.

Darren and Jock exit. Doink begins to follow Darren.

Tracy (*to Doink*) What's your real name?

Pause.

Doink Terry.

Pause.

Tracy Terry?

Pause.

So where'd you get Doink from?

Doink Dunno.

Pause.

Tracy Off you go then. Wouldn't want you missin a hot date with an octopus.

Pause.

Doink You'd know all about hot dates.

Tracy What?

Doink Nothin.

Tracy (*sits up*) What did you say?

Doink Just somethin I heard.

43

Tracy From who?

Doink About you bein in a bit of trouble.

Tracy What did he say?

Doink Who?

Tracy Darren.

Doink Who's talkin about Darren?

Tracy lies back down.

Tracy I hear you're havin a bit of trouble with your octopus.

Doink No.

Pause.

What's wrong is that some spics round here are comin in here an takin what's ours.

Tracy You'll have to sort that out.

Doink I'm plannin on sortin it. Startin tomorrow at school. Anti-English day?

Tracy That sounds like fun.

Pause.

Doink You ain't been here long but you'll soon find out what the spics really think of us.

Tracy You better go an kill somethin then. Get in trainin.

Doink Your brother's lookin forward to it. (*Begins to walk away.*) He's a good bloke, your brother.

Pause.

Tracy Darren ain't goin to school tomorrow.

Doink stops.

Doink (*walks back to Tracy*) What?

Tracy I said Darren ain't goin to school tomorrow.

Doink Why?

Tracy (*sits up*) He ain't told you?

Doink No.

Tracy My mum's keepin him off.

Doink She can't keep him off.

Tracy She wrote a letter into the school.

　Pause.

Doink He's gotta go in.

Tracy Why?

Doink He gotta.

　Pause.

It's anti-English day.

Tracy It's stupid is what it is.

Doink It's his . . .

Tracy What?

Doink . . . his duty.

　Pause.

Tracy Don't try an drag my brother into some stupid little game.

SCENE FOUR

4 May 1982. Rosia Bay.

Doink and Jock run onstage. They stop, out of breath.
They are elated, but scared. Both are wearing sta-prest
trousers. Jock is wearing a Fred Perry T-shirt and Doc
Martens, Doink is wearing an Adidas T-shirt and
trainers.

Jock Fuckin hell.

Doink looks as though he thinks they are being
chased. He looks behind them.

What is it?

Pause.

Doink S'alright.

Jock Fuckin hell.

Doink That was fuckin amazin.

Jock We're in the shit.

Doink Fuckin brilliant.

Jock We're in so much shit, mate.

Doink That was the best though, weren't it?

Jock I dunno.

Doink See the way they fuckin run.

Pause.

Jock He's a nutter, that Kev. Takin a knife.

Doink They fuckin ran when they saw him cut one of
them. Fuckin shat themselves.

Jock He's mental.

Doink He's alright.

Pause.

I was gonna take my knife. You know what spics are like for knives, the wankers.

Jock They didn't have any knives.

Doink I knew I should have taken my knife.

Pause.

Typical spics though innit. Can't fuckin fight fair. Supposed to be one on one, best English fighter, best spic fighter. Fuckin spic brings all his brothers along.

Jock And we all went along with Kev.

Doink Cos we knew what they were gonna do. (*He begins to jump about in front of Jock.*) I was right behind Kev, shoutin come on you spic cunts, let's be havin you. Did you see me?

Jock No. I couldn't get near the front.

Doink Oh mate. I was right there. It was fuckin brilliant. I decked this spic. He was fuckin massive. Knocked him right on his fuckin arse. D'you see that?

Jock No . . . I must've missed that an all.

Doink It was the fuckin best. Chasin them all over their own flats. They were bangin on the doors to get away. Who was that kid who chucked the brick? Through the window?

Jock Dunno. Some Army kid.

Doink It was so fuckin funny. That old spic geezer looked out his window to see what was goin on and, bosh. That kid throws a brick right through it.

Jock Yeah.

47

Doink Him comin out with his walkin stick and tryin to whack everybody.

Jock He was so old he could barely lift it up.

Doink What about the women? When they all come runnin out their houses, screamin at us?

Jock Yeah.

Doink The women are scarier than the men.

Jock Hairier.

They both laugh.

Doink Steve would have loved that today.

Pause.

He won't be the only one with a few stories when he comes back.

Pause.

That'll make them think twice about comin down here.

Pause.

Jock What d'you wanna do now?

Doink I ain't goin home.

Jock Fuck that.

Doink If we're in the shit it can wait.

Jock We're in the shit.

Doink (*laughs*) It was our last anti-English day, you gotta make it a good one.

Pause.

Can't believe that little fucker Darren didn't come in. Wanker. I knew he didn't have the bottle.

Jock It ain't his fault.

Pause.

Doink Didn't think you were gonna go over the flats.

Jock I thought it was a trap. Get us in the middle an then there'd be loads of them all waitin.

Pause.

I went, didn't I?

Doink I thought you were gonna bottle it.

Jock Don't be daft.

Doink Thought you were shittin it.

Jock I wasn't shittin it.

Doink Thought for a moment you wished you'd stayed at home with Darren.

Jock Piss off.

Doink You've been actin like you'd rather be hangin about with spics ever since you started playin football with them.

Jock No I ain't.

Doink Yeah, you have.

Pause.

Jock It's all right for you.

Doink What?

Jock You're leavin.

Doink You're leavin too.

Jock I ain't talkin about school.

Doink What then?

Pause.

Jock You'll be goin in the Marines.

Doink So are you.

Jock Yeah, but I gotta wait till I'm eighteen.

Doink Your mum an dad ain't gonna let you go this year?

Jock I tried to persuade them. But they just won't let me. Me old boy reckons I won't wanna go in by then. Once I've worked for a couple of years an that.

Pause.

It's me that'll be left here. I've been here five years and we still don't know when we'll be leavin.

Pause.

Feels like home to me, this.

Doink You're a Jock.

Jock Yeah. Well, I don't feel like it.

Doink Yeah.

Jock I can hardly remember livin there. I go on holiday an I'm like . . . it's a fuckin shithole.

Doink And this ain't a shithole?

Jock Yeah.

Pause.

At least it's hot.

Pause.

Doink Can't believe you went in wearin Docs.

Jock (*looks down at his feet*) For scrappin.

Doink Yeah. But come on. Docs? Fuckin embarassin. It's like all them spics with their bikers' boots an that. You gonna start likin all that greaser music. Start fuckin headbangin.

Pause.

Jock When d'you get them?

Doink (*looking at his trainers*) Nice, ain't they?

Jock They're alright.

Doink Smart.

Jock Spoiled, you are.

Tracy enters.

Tracy He said you'd be down here.

Pause.

Come on, Darren.

Darren enters.

Jock Alright, mate.

Doink No, he fuckin isn't alright.

Pause.

Where the fuck were you today?

Darren I was . . .

Doink Suppose you heard what happened?

Darren Yeah.

Pause.

Sorry.

Doink You should be fuckin sorry.

Tracy Everyone's been lookin for you.

Jock I fuckin knew we were in the shit.

Doink You let your fuckin mates down today.

Darren I'm sorry.

Doink You fuckin knew we needed everybody. You knew what was gonna happen.

Darren Yeah, and my mum knew what was gonna happen.

Doink Everyone's mum knew what was gonna fuckin happen. My old girl said get in there an give them hell. All the Army kids got told they'd be lettin the regiment down if they didn't go in. Their bus never even turned up an they all walked in.

    Pause.

It were fuckin brilliant. Weren't it, Jock?

Tracy He said you might have come down here, when you heard.

Doink Heard?

Darren When you heard what happened.

Doink Listen to him, Jock. Fuckin believe him. When you heard. We were fuckin there, you tosser.

Darren Not school.

Doink We don't let our mates down.

Tracy You ain't heard.

Jock What?

    Pause.

Tracy (*to Doink*) You ain't heard yet, have you?

Jock We ain't heard what?

Doink What's goin on?

Tracy You better go home, Doink.

Doink I ain't goin anywhere till someone tells me what's fuckin goin on.

Pause.

Darren The Argies.

Doink What about the fuckin Argies?

Tracy They sunk the *Sheffield*.

SCENE FIVE

6 May 1982. Rosia Bay.
Jock and Tracy are sitting together on the wall.

Tracy Ten.

Jock Don't matter.

Tracy How many have you been to?

Jock How many houses have you lived in?

Tracy How many schools?

Jock It's not schools. It's houses.

Tracy How many?

Jock Houses?

Tracy Schools.

Pause.

How many?

Jock counts on his hands.

You gonna have to use your toes as well.

Jock I've lost count now.

Tracy One school a year nearly.

Jock (*counting again*) Seven.

Tracy I win.

Jock How many houses?

Tracy I dunno. But it figures if I've been to more schools, I've lived in more houses.

> *Pause.*

It must be nice stayin in one place. Not movin all the time. Havin friends.

Jock Yeah.

> *Pause.*

Tracy Here's OK, I reckon.

Jock Yeah. It ain't bad.

Tracy I think I could do somethin here.

Jock What?

Tracy I dunno. Somethin.

Jock Yeah.

> *Pause.*

Tracy What about you? I know you do all that runnin about stuff, but you've got more sense than wantin to join the Marines.

Jock Yeah. I have.

> *Pause.*

I wanna join the Paras.

54

Tracy laughs.

Tracy Don't none of you want to do nothin else?

Jock Doink reckons it's adventure. I just reckon it's all gonna be more of the same. I ain't allowed to go till I'm eighteen anyway. So I'm stuck here for a couple more years.

Pause.

Suppose you get used to movin.

Tracy Some people do.

Pause.

Darren hates it.

Jock No?

Pause.

Tracy He really likes you two. All he talks about is gettin a speargun and goin divin.

Jock He should get one then.

Tracy You're jokin. He ain't got a chance. There's no way my mum'll let him get one. She thinks they're too dangerous. She thinks you two are dangerous.

Pause.

Tracy How is he?

Jock Doink?

Tracy Yeah.

Jock Alright.

Pause.

Tracy There ain't much chance his brother's been hurt.

Jock Yeah.

Tracy There was only twenty got killed.

Jock Yeah. We got hundreds on the *Belgrano*.

Tracy Three hundred or somethin.

> *Pause.*

Jock Gonna have to be really unlucky. Steve. Doink.

> *Pause.*

Tracy You ever been bullied?

Jock Everybody gets bullied.

Tracy No they don't.

Jock Yeah they do.

> *Pause.*

Tracy Darren used to get bullied bad at home.

Jock Yeah?

Tracy Really bad.

> *Pause.*

Don't tell him I told you.

Jock I won't.

Tracy I just don't want it to happen to him again.

Jock Doink ain't a bully.

Tracy He better not be.

Jock He's alright, you know.

Tracy Yeah?

> *Pause.*

What are you two gonna do today?

Jock Dunno. He just said I was to meet him. He had a surprise for me.

Tracy A surprise?

Jock Yeah.

Pause.

Tracy You couldn't take Darren along?

Jock I dunno.

Tracy He really likes you two.

Jock I know, but . . . Doink.

Tracy You just said he's alright.

Jock Yeah.

Tracy So it'll be alright?

Pause.

Jock Yeah.

Tracy (*kisses Jock on the cheek*) I knew you were one of the good ones.

Jock He's a good bloke.

Tracy He hides it pretty well.

Pause.

Jock Steve. His brother, yeah. He's a brilliant bloke. He'll do anythin. He's good at everythin. Football, swimmin, fightin. Doink ain't so good at stuff. Cept fightin. He's good at fightin.

Tracy Well, that's somethin.

Jock It's better than nothin.

Pause.

57

Tracy Cojones.

Jock laughs.

That's what's wrong with you blokes. Too many bollocks.

Jock laughs.

Jock *Huevos.*

Tracy *Huevos?*

Jock *Huevos.* Eggs.

Tracy Eggs?

Jock (*cups his hand*) *Heuvos.* That's what spics, Gibraltarians say as well. Like the slang.

Tracy D'you speak Spanish, then?

Jock Nearly.

Tracy Nearly?

Jock Yeah.

Tracy How can you nearly speak a language?

Pause.

Jock I can do the swearin.

Tracy laughs.

I'm fuckin good at it.

Doink enters. He has a new, compressed-air speargun cradled in his hand.

Alright, mate? Fuckin hell. When d'you get that? Give us a look.

Doink hands the gun to Jock.

That is a fuckin nice gun.

Pause.

Tracy (*to Doink*) Alright?

Doink Yeah. Fine.

Jock (*aims the gun around*) You're gonna catch so much with that.

Tracy Don't point that at me.

Jock Compressed-air, this.

Tracy They give me the creeps.

Pause.

How's your mum?

Doink Fine. (*to Jock*) She just went out an bought it for me. Thought she would have forgotten.

Jock Lucky bastard.

Pause.

Tracy (*she touches Doink's arm*) You OK?

Doink Why shouldn't I be?

Pause.

Jock (*holds up the speargun*) You gonna let us see this thing in action?

Doink I ain't firin it here.

Jock Fire it into a bit of wood or somethin.

Doink I ain't firin it into any wood.

Jock I'll find a bit.

Jock begins looking around for a piece of wood.

Doink It'll stick in wood. We won't be able to get it out.

Jock This wood's all rotten. It ain't gonna stick in rotten wood. (*Jock holds up a piece of wood.*) Here's a nice bit.

Doink joins Jock and looks at the piece of wood.

Doink It don't look very rotten.

Jock (*stands the lump of wood on end*) It's perfect.

Doink It'll get stuck.

Jock It'll be alright. Just imagine it's a spic.

Doink raises his gun and aims at the wood.

Doink Stand back.

Doink fires the speargun.

Jock Fuckin hell.

Tracy Jesus.

Jock runs to the spear and begins to prise it from the wood.

Jock The fuckin power in that.

Doink (*to Tracy*) How's your brother?

Tracy He's alright.

Pause.

What are you two gonna do?

Doink I wanna go trainin. Go for a run.

Jock Yeah?

Doink Yeah.

Jock Alright.

Tracy Darren was talkin about wantin to go trainin.

Jock Yeah?

Tracy Yeah.

Pause.

Jock Tell him to come out and get us, yeah.

Tracy Yeah?

Jock Yeah. (*to Doink*) That'd be alright won't it, mate?

Pause.

Doink Yeah. (*to Tracy*) Tell him it's alright.

Tracy Alright. Cheers.

Tracy exits.

Doink Spoke to anyone? About school? About Kev?

Jock The police got him in town.

Doink What's gonna happen?

Jock Dunno.

Doink They'll send him back to England. Look after their own. The Army.

Pause.

Jock Hundred stitches I heard.

Doink Who?

Jock The spic.

Pause.

Doink Deserved it Argie-lovin spic bastard.

Pause.

You ain't seen any of your spic mates?

Jock They ain't my mates now.

Doink Good.

Pause.

You an me, we're goin down to Rosia tonight.

Jock Look for some occies.

Doink Look for some spics.

Jock Oh come on, mate.

Doink What?

Jock Them nickin a couple of occies is the least of your problems now.

Pause.

Doink I've got booze.

Jock Yeah?

Pause.

Doink You're all mates with her, then?

Jock She was just askin about you.

Doink Yeah?

Jock I reckon you could be in there.

Pause.

You don't mind Darren comin along?

Doink (*takes the speargun back from Jock*) No, mate. I've got plans for him.

Jock What?

Doink Take him on the run.

Jock Yeah.

Doink Give him a fuckin beatin.

Jock Come on, mate.

Doink Bit of payback for school.

Jock He's still one of us.

Doink Is he?

   Pause.

Five clicks, yeah.

Jock Five?

Doink Up an down five times.

   Pause.

See if the little poof can hack that.

SCENE SIX

A path above Rosia Bay.
   Doink, Jock and Darren are running. They have their diver's bags on their backs with the straps over their shoulders to approximate military rucksacks. Jock's speargun is over his shoulder. Darren is dressed in an approximate way to Jock and Doink, with a pack but without a T-shirt and with a Rambo-style headband. He stops running.

Darren (*panting*) I've got a stitch.

   Doink and Jock also stop running.

Doink Can't fuckin hack it.

Darren It's steep this hill, ain't it?

Jock Just don't think about it, Darren.

Doink (*shouting*) Move, you horrible little man.

   Jock starts laughing. Doink begins to pull him along by the strap on his pack.

Shift.

Darren surprises Doink by wrestling himself free.

Darren It's really hot. Why we doin this in the middle of the day?

Doink Cos it's harder.

Darren Be better at night or in the mornin.

Doink Too easy.

Darren We're gonna get sunstroke.

Doink No you ain't.

Darren Don't you think it's hot, Jock?

Jock It's alright.

Doink tries to pull Darren along again. Darren pulls himself free again.

Darren (*feeling his shoulder*) It's the straps on this pack. They're hurtin my shoulders.

Doink The straps on your fuckin bra.

Jock (*to Darren*) What's up with the pack?

Doink That ain't a pack. I dunno what it is but it ain't no fuckin pack.

Darren It's cuttin into my shoulders.

Doink Tough.

Jock Hold them with your hands.

Darren I have been. It just hurts me hands. (*Darren takes his pack off.*)

Doink You can't fuckin hack it, mate.

Darren I can hack it. (*He points at his shoulder.*) Look at that.

Doink ignores Darren. Jock goes to him and looks at his shoulder.

Jock It ain't very red.

Darren It's sore.

Doink You better go an show your mum. Get a fuckin note. Poof.

Darren I'm gonna have blisters.

Jock (*examining Darren's pack*) Where d'you get this, Daz?

Darren Me mum made it.

Jock Your fuckin mum made it.

Darren I told her I was comin trainin with you two and I needed a pack to run with an she made me this.

Jock That's an old shopping bag.

Darren I dunno.

Jock And that's a skippin rope.

Darren It's the straps.

Doink It's a girl's skippin rope.

Jock It's pink.

Darren It ain't pink.

Doink Yeah it is.

Darren Skippin's good trainin. Boxers skip. (*Darren sits down on the ground.*)

Doink On your feet.

Jock stands Darren up.

Darren This is the furthest we've run.

Doink Yeah, and we're keepin goin.

Darren I ain't.

Doink We're doin five clicks today. With no rests.

Darren I gotta sort this pack out.

Doink You can sort it out at the end.

Darren How far we done?

Doink About three.

Darren It's further than that.

Doink It ain't. This is our third time goin up.

Darren It's the fourth, innit?

Doink It's the third. You know it's the third.

Darren It's the fourth.

Doink Get movin.

Darren I'm stayin here.

Doink Move.

Doink tries to pull Darren along.

Move.

Darren Fuck off.

Doink grabs Darren. Jock pulls him off.

Jock Leave him, Doink.

Doink Fuckin tell me to fuck off.

Jock If he can't do it, he can't do it. It don't fuckin matter.

Darren Yeah. It ain't me that's joinin the Paras.

Doink The fuckin Paras? Who the fuck's joinin the Paras?

Darren indicates Jock.

Doink (*to Jock*) You're comin in the Marines.

Jock Yeah.

Darren (*to Jock*) When we were talking the other day you said you were thinkin about the Paras.

Doink Fuckin hell.

Jock What?

Doink Why d'you want to join them fuckin idiots?

Jock I dunno.

Doink Fuckin hell. (*Doink snatches the headband from Darren's head.*) What the fuck is this?

Jock Come on Doink. Lay off him.

Doink Lay off him?

Darren It's a headband.

Doink I know what it fuckin is. Why?

Darren There's this film, yeah, *First Blood*. I got a pirate copy of it. It's that Sylvester Stallone. He's called Rambo in it.

Jock I heard about that.

Darren It's really good. I'll lend you the video. You as well, Doink. It's dead good.

Doink turns and punches Darren, knocking him off his feet.

Jock (*grabs Doink*) Doink.

Doink pushes Jock away and kicks and punches Darren.

Doink Fuckin Rambo. You think watchin somethin like that makes you hard? Where the fuck d'you get off?

There's fuckin people dyin down there for real an you're wankin over a fuckin video. My brother's in a war an he's gonna have to come back here an listen to little wankers like you goin on about Rambo. (*Doink finishes the beating and turns to Jock.*) Little fuckin poof. Can't hack it. Ain't got the guts. Just like he ain't got the guts to go to school on anti-English day. (*to Darren*) You ain't got the guts for nothin.

Doink throws the headband at Darren as he's lying on the ground. Doink exits.

Jock (*helping Darren to his feet*) Come on, mate. (*He points to the pack.*) You should've put a T-shirt on. Stopped it rubbin.

Darren (*looks at his shoulders*) I wanted to start gettin a tan.

Jock You got a towel?

Darren Yeah.

Jock Put your towel round your shoulders. Now put your pack on. That'll stop the rubbin.

Darren does as Jock tells him.

That better?

Darren Yeah.

Jock picks up Darren's headband.

Jock It does look a bit stupid.

Darren starts crying.

There's no point fuckin cryin, mate. Cryin ain't gonna do you any fuckin good.

Darren What have I done?

Jock (*shrugs*) Nothin.

Darren It ain't my fault if I ain't as fit as him.

Pause.

I wanted to go to school . . .

Jock It ain't that. Not any more.

Pause.

Close. Steve and Doink.

Darren Yeah. But he's probably alright.

Jock Still.

Darren There's only twenty dead.

Jock Till they know, yeah . . .

Pause.

Let's get goin then.

Darren What?

Jock You ain't stoppin.

Darren Ain't I?

Jock No. Cos we're gonna, you're gonna show Doink what you can do today, Darren. You're gonna show him you can hack it.

Darren I can't hack it.

Jock You can.

Darren He hates me.

Jock But he'll know you did five miles. It's the only way to do it. You gotta show people you can do it. You got two choices in life. You can lie down an get kicked or you can stand an fight. Now you're gonna show him. Today. Alright?

Darren (*shaking his head*) No.

Jock (*grabs hold of Darren*) You are. No point in sittin on the ground an cryin, feelin sorry for yourself. You gotta stand on your own two feet, mate. You can't fuckin hide behind your mum and your sister.

Darren I don't.

Jock Yeah. Well it looks that way to Doink.

    Pause.

Listen. I know. About what happened to you before.

Darren What?

    Pause.

Jock Gettin bullied an that.

Darren I never.

Jock It's OK, mate.

Darren I didn't.

Jock Nothin to be ashamed of.

    Darren pulls himself free from Jock and runs off.

Darren.

    Pause.

Fuck.

SCENE SEVEN

Rosia Bay. Night.
    Doink and Jock sit on the wall looking out to sea. They are dresed as they were in the afternoon, with all their snorkelling gear in bags. They are both smoking and drinking from bottles of lager.

Jock I reckon that Tracy . . .

Doink What about her?

Jock I . . . I reckon . . . you could be in there.

Doink She's a fuckin slag, mate.

Jock That's what I mean.

Doink What?

Jock That's what you want. No point in chasin some spic bird. They won't let you do nothin. It's like that Nancy . . .

Doink Who?

Jock That Nancy, from down at . . .

Doink Fuckin hell. How old is she?

Jock I dunno.

Doink Twelve?

Jock She's about fourteen.

Doink She ain't fuckin fourteen.

Jock She is.

Doink Twelve tops. She looks about ten.

Jock She's at the girls' comp.

Doink No way is she at the girls' comp. You're a kiddy-fiddler, you.

Jock Fuck off.

Doink Did you shag her?

   Pause.

Did you?

Jock Why d'you wanna know?

Doink I was wonderin is all.

Jock So you can have a wank over it?

Pause.

Doink So did you shag her?

Jock Shut up.

Doink So what you do with her? You finger her?

Jock Course I did.

Doink She bald?

Jock Fuck off.

Doink Couldn't you get it up when she was bald?

Jock (*laughing*) Fuck off.

Doink Or was she too tight?

Pause.

Jock She wouldn't let me.

Doink You're too fuckin ugly, mate.

Pause.

Get her drunk. That's the best way . . . Get them drunk
an then they'll do anythin, that's what Steve says.

> *Doink gets up and moves away. He drinks from his
> bottle before throwing it into the sea. Doink keeps his
> back to Jock. Jock finishes his bottle of lager and picks
> up a large bottle of Coke. He removes the cap and
> drinks from it.*

Jock Fuck me, that's strong.

Pause.

72

Doink Never used rum before.

Jock (*takes another, longer drink*) It ain't bad actually.

Doink (*turns back round and takes the bottle of Coke from Jock*) You ain't drinkin all of it. (*Doink drinks from the bottle.*) Jesus.

Jock It's good, innit?

Doink (*taking another drink*) That little poof Darren was funny today.

Jock Yeah.

  Pause.

You were pretty hard on him, mate.

Doink And?

Jock Nothin. (*Jock takes the bottle back and continues drinking.*) Remember that time we jumped off the hundred-ton gun.

Doink Remember it. I was pickin me speedos out me crack for a week.

Jock I told you to wear cut-offs.

Doink Thought I was gonna have to go up the Naval Hospital an have an operation. Get them cut out.

Jock It was fuckin high.

Doink That why you wanna join the Paras, cos you like jumpin off things?

Jock No.

Doink So what was that all about this afternoon?

Jock Just that little Darren wanker mouthin off.

Doink The fuckin Paras.

  Pause.

Jock Jumpin off the gun though. No one else has done that. Not even your Steve or the older lads.

Doink They weren't daft enough.

Jock Remember the bollockin he gave us after we done it?

Doink I thought he was gonna kill me.

Jock He couldn't catch me.

Pause.

Doink He was proud though.

Jock Yeah.

Doink I could tell.

Pause.

I always thought we were gonna stick together.

Jock We have stuck together, mate.

Doink There was like Steve an his mates an like you an me. We were the only two young lads they ever let hang about with them.

Jock Everyone else was wankers.

Doink No they weren't. Just we were . . . we were better.

Pause.

Now. You ain't comin in the Marines with me?

Jock I told you, I can't get my dad to give me permission.

Pause.

Doink I'm gonna be on my own.

Pause.

Jock We've had some laughs though. (*Takes the bottle and drinks.*) We fuckin ruled this place.

Pause.

Doink And we're leavin it to wankers like that Darren.

Jock It don't matter. We ain't gonna be here.

Doink Don't mean we have to give it to the spics.

Jock I don't think they give a toss, mate.

Doink How do you know? They might come down here tonight.

Jock They won't

Doink How d'you know?

Tracy enters. She is wearing a T-shirt, jeans and trainers.

Jock Fuckin hell.

Tracy Have you two seen Darren?

Jock We was just talkin about you.

Tracy Oh yeah?

Doink About your brother.

Tracy Do you know where he is?

Jock No.

Tracy What you on about then?

Doink He's a bit pissed.

Jock No I ain't.

Jock offers the bottle to Tracy.

Tracy (*shakes her head*) Have you seen Darren?

Jock No.

Doink He gone missin again, has he?

Tracy I ain't pissin about. D'you know where he is?

Doink No.

Tracy I thought he might be down here. He hasn't come home since he came out to meet you two.

Doink (*takes the bottle and has a drink*) Haven't seen him since this afternoon.

Jock He'll be alright.

Tracy It ain't like him, though.

Doink It's not like you can run away in a place this size. Nowhere to run, is there?

Jock He'll be alright.

   Pause.

Tracy (*to Doink*) You didn't say anythin to him about school?

Doink No.

Tracy He couldn't help not goin into school, you know.

Doink We went for a run and then he went off. Didn't he, Jock?

   Jock takes a drink.

Doink (*takes the bottle*) Dunno where he went.

Tracy It weren't his fault. School. If you knew our mum.

Jock Is she anythin like you?

Tracy No. She don't half go on.

   Jock and Doink laugh.

What?

Doink Nothin.

76

Jock and Doink keep giggling.

Tracy What are you two laughin at?

Doink Nothin.

Tracy What?

Doink It's him. He's pissed.

Tracy (*to Jock*) You better not be takin the piss out of me.

Jock I ain't.

Doink Why would he do that, you're his new mate?

Pause.

Tracy Seriously. I need to find Darren. He's done this before.

Doink Anti-English day.

Tracy No. (*to Jock*) I told you, didn't I?

Jock Yeah.

Pause.

Doink (*to Jock*) What?

Jock takes a very long drink.

Tracy Darren used to get really bullied at home.

Doink Yeah.

Tracy Yeah. And I don't just mean a bit of name-callin an stuff. Kids' stuff. I mean really bad stuff. Really bad beatins an stuff.

Pause.

Doink He'll turn up.

Jock gets up unsteadily and offers the bottle to Tracy.

Tracy (*taking the bottle*) What is it?

Jock Rum.

Doink And Coke.

> *Tracy wipes the top of the bottle before taking a very long drink.*

Tracy Needs more rum.

> *Doink laughs. Jock takes a long drink from the bottle and lights another cigarette.*

Is this the only place you hang about?

Doink No.

Jock Yeah.

> *Pause.*

Tracy Don't you ever go out anywhere?

Doink This is out.

Tracy I mean out.

Doink It's alright for girls, innit? You get in anywhere. If you're a bloke they're always askin for a warrant card.

> *Jock stands up. He is very drunk.*

Jock I was just thinkin. (*He looks for the bottle, picks it up and drinks from it. To Tracy*) I ran away.

Tracy You what?

Jock (*takes another long drink*) I ran away.

Doink When?

Jock I did.

Doink When.

Jock Years ago. (*Jock takes another long drink.*)

Tracy Where d'you go?

Jock (*thinks*) Away.

> *Doink begins laughing.*

Far away.

> *Tracy begins laughing. Jock joins in the laughter. He leans back with the bottle in his hand and lying on the wall, slips into unconsciousness.*

Tracy (*takes the bottle from Jock's hand*) I'll be havin that. (*She takes a drink and hands the bottle to Doink.*) You'd think he could handle his drink better, bein a Jock.

Doink He'll be alright.

Tracy I hope so.

Doink He does it all the time. One minute he's OK, the next he's . . .

> *Pause.*

I once found him unconscious in a, like an oil drum, full of sangria. At a party.

> *Tracy laughs.*

It was lucky I had my lifesavin badge.

Tracy Did you do mouth-to-mouth?

Doink No. Just like hit him on the back and stuff.

> *Pause.*

Tracy Don't you do mouth-to-mouth, then?

> *Pause.*

Doink You're always takin the piss.

Tracy Yeah.

Doink gets up and begins to put Jock in the recovery position.

Doink I met him the first day we come here. We lived down at Tower an he just come up an said hello an that was it.

Pause.

He's been out here so long he don't know what he is. Spic or British or a Jock or what.

Tracy He's a boy is what he is.

Pause.

Doink He's me oppo.

Tracy picks up the bottle and drinks from it. She hands it to Doink. Doink takes it and Tracy touches his hand. She traces her hand across his fingers and onto his wrist.

Tracy You got a really good tan.

Doink Yeah.

Tracy Like a spic, you are.

Doink Shut up.

Pause.

Tracy Why d'you wanna join the Army?

Doink Marines is Navy.

Pause. Shrugs.

What else is there?

Tracy Suppose.

Doink (*to Tracy*) And what are you gonna do?

Tracy Dunno.

Pause.

I might stay here.

Doink Fuckin shithole, this place.

Tracy Good weather.

Pause.

I like the sun.

Doink Me dad says, if you're from Pompey you've only got three choices. You can work in the dockyard, join the Navy, go in the Marines. Me dad works in the yard, my brother's . . .

Pause.

I'm gonna join the Marines. Completes the set.

Pause.

Tracy You know, they say there's three things you've gotta be to be a Marine. You've gotta be strong as a carthorse, fast as a racehorse, and thick as a rockin horse.

Pause.

You can't join them, see. You ain't thick.

Doink Ain't I?

Tracy No you ain't.

Pause.

Soft's what you are.

Pause.

Doink Steve's dead.

Tracy What?

Doink Found out this mornin.

Pause.

I'm alright.

Pause.

I couldn't stay in the house.

Pause.

I shoulda done. I know. But . . . me mum . . .

Doink turns away from Tracy. Tracy moves towards Doink and puts her arm round him.

Tracy It's alright.

Doink How can they sink the *Sheffield*?

Tracy It's OK.

Doink The fuckin Argies, though? They're fuckin shit. A fuckin joke. Everyone says. They can't fight us. They don't have a chance. We were gonna murder them. Best in the world we are.

Doink begins to cry. Tracy puts her arm round him.

Doink We dunno if there's even gonna be a funeral.

Pause.

I keep thinkin about him down here. Mouthin off. Takin the piss. He ruled this place.

Pause.

Me mum wants to get him back home. Doesn't want him lyin down there in the sea. Freezin, she says.

Tracy kisses Doink. Doink pulls away.

Doink Don't feel sorry for me.

Tracy I don't. (*She moves towards him.*) Come here. (*She kisses Doink again. She takes his hand.*) What happened to your hand?

Doink Nothin.

Tracy You been fightin again.

Pause.

Doink It's nothin.

Tracy (*she kisses Doink's hand*) He says you're good at fightin.

Doink shrugs.

There's better things to be good at. (*She puts his hand on her breast.*) You good at anythin else?

Tracy kisses Doink. As they kiss she pushes Doink onto his back. Doink flips her over so he's on top, pinning her to the ground. They kiss.

(*trying to push him off*) Hang on a minute.

Doink moves against her sexually. Tracy tries to push him off.

Let me get me jeans off.

Doink kisses her. He continues to grind against her. He breathes heavily. He shakes. He ejaculates. He collapses. He rolls away from her. Tracy sits up.

Tracy Terry.

Doink (*pushes her away*) Go an find your brother.

Darren enters.

Tracy Darren.

Darren stares down at Doink.

(*Gets up.*) Where have you been?

Darren (*to Doink*) You alright?

Tracy How long have you been here?

Darren stares down at Doink.

Doink (*standing up*) What are you doin down here?

Tracy (*to Darren*) Where have you been?

Darren (*to Doink*) You alright?

Doink Yeah. Where have you been?

Darren I've been down here.

Doink You been fuckin spyin on us?

Darren Keepin an eye on things.

Doink Fuckin spyin.

Tracy (*to Doink*) Shut up.

Darren (*to Doink*) I ain't spyin on anyone.

Tracy pulls Darren away from Jock and Doink.

Tracy Are you alright?

Darren Yeah.

Tracy What happened to your face?

Darren I'm fine.

Tracy Darren? (*to Doink*) Look at him.

Doink Yeah.

Pause.

What happened, mate?

Tracy Have you been fightin?

Darren No.

Tracy Where have you been?

Darren I just went off for a bit.

Tracy Where?

Darren I just went off. (*to Doink*) I've been thinkin about things.

Tracy What things?

   Pause.

Darren You're a fuckin slag, sis.

Tracy What?

Darren I saw you.

   Pause.

You're like all of them. You think you know everythin an tell people what to do an say, you want to help us an then you tell people about what happened to me. You're full of shit.

Tracy It wasn't like that . . .

Darren It ain't what people say, it's what they do that matters. (*Points to his face.*) You were right to do this to me?

Tracy (*to Doink*) Did you do that to his face?

Darren What you doin with her?

Tracy (*to Darren*) Why did he hit you?

Darren I deserved it.

Tracy (*to Doink*) Why didn't you tell me where he was?

Doink I didn't know where he was.

Tracy You knew what had happened. Why didn't you say somethin?

   Pause.

Why are you doin this?

Doink He's gotta fuckin learn.

Pause.

He's gotta learn.

Tracy How to be a man?

Pause.

I know you can't show him how to do that.

Pause.

Apologise to him.

Pause.

Apologise to him.

Doink Will you fuck off if I do?

Pause.

(*to Darren*) Sorry.

Darren S'alright.

Tracy No it ain't. (*to Darren*) We better get home.

Darren (*to Doink*) You ain't got nothin to be sorry for.

Tracy Darren.

Darren (*to Tracy*) Go home.

Doink Yeah. Why don't you fuck off?

Tracy exits.

Darren (*to Doink*) Listen, mate. I was thinkin about what you said though. I ain't gonna ever let my mates down again. You gotta stick by your mates. You let someone take the piss then everyone takes the piss.

Doink (*puts his face as close as he can to Darren's face*) You're takin the fuckin piss?

Darren No.

Doink (*to Darren*) You're full of fuckin shit, mate.

Darren Not any more.

Doink All fuckin mouth.

Doink walks away from Darren. Darren is distracted by something in the sea.

Darren Doink.

Doink Fuck off.

Darren There's someone in the water over there.

Doink stops and looks at Darren.

I mean it.

Doink climbs the wall and looks out to sea.

Over there.

Doink watches.

(*pointing*) Over there.

Doink Jock.

Pause.

Jock. Wake up.

Jock doesn't move. Doink climbs down from the wall.

Doink (*shaking Jock*) Wake up, mate.

Darren climbs down from the wall.

Jock (*jumps awake*) What the fuck?

Doink It's the spics.

Jock What?

Doink In the water.

Jock What?

Doink Spics.

Doink opens his bag and begins pulling out his wetsuit.

Jock (*to Doink*) What you doin?

Doink (*starts to take off his clothes*) Spics.

Jock (*jumps up*) Where?

Doink In the water.

Jock climbs up the wall and looks out to sea.

See the light?

Jock Yeah.

Doink (*picks up his speargun*) This is it. It's up to us.

Jock What you gonna do with that?

Doink Scare him off. Show them they can't come down here.

Jock Fuck's sake, mate.

Darren (*to Doink*) I'll do it.

Doink Piss off.

Darren I will.

Doink ignores Darren.

Darren Please, Doink.

Pause.

Doink How long were you watchin anyway?

Darren (*standing in front of Doink*) Give me the gun.

Doink That how you get your kicks is it, watchin your sister on the job? Fuckin coward. Fuckin pervert. No wonder you get fuckin bullied. (*Pushes Darren out of the way.*) Fuck off.

Darren picks up Doink's speargun.

Darren I ain't scared.

Doink lunges for Darren, who evades him and points the gun at him. Doink backs away.

Why won't you let me? I can hack it.

Doink No you fuckin can't.

Darren I ain't scared.

Doink Yeah you fuckin are.

Jock Doink.

Darren I've been thinkin about all the things you said. You need me, Doink.

Doink No I fuckin don't.

Darren We've all gotta stick together.

Darren I can do it.

Doink Go on then.

Jock Doink.

Darren Fuckin show the fuckin lot of you.

Jock Darren.

Darren Fuckin spic bastards.

Darren stands on the wall and turns towards the sea. Darren fires the speargun.

SCENE EIGHT

22 May 1982. Rosia Bay.
  Darren, Jock and Doink are preparing to go
spearfishing.

Darren It's fuckin hot innit?

Doink It's gettin there, mate, it's gettin there.

Darren Reckon I could get used to this.

Doink You will, mate, you will.

  Pause.

Darren (*to Jock*) What d'you reckon we'll get today?

Jock Dunno, mate.

Darren I reckon there might be a few big fuckers about.

Doink I hope so.

Darren (*to Jock*) Gotta get earnin, ain't we, occy-eyes?

  Pause.

Jock Yeah.

Darren There's gotta be a few about. There won't have
been no one sniffin around since . . .

  Pause.

It's good to get out.

  Pause.

Jock (*to Darren*) Your sister spoke to you yet?

Darren No chance.

Jock She ain't speakin to us neither.

Pause.

(*to Darren*) She alright?

Darren (*shrugs*) Dunno.

Pause.

I was goin spare in the house.

Jock Me too.

Darren I thought they were never gonna leave me on me own ever again. Felt like a fuckin prisoner. You'd think it was the fuckin Queen, not just some fuckin spic.

Jock Don't say that, mate.

Pause.

Doink I'm surprised you got out so quick.

Darren Yeah.

Pause.

What they gonna do? Chain me up?

Pause.

What've you been up to, Doink?

Doink Nothin much. Trainin an that.

Darren Not long to go now.

Doink Yeah.

Pause.

I can't wait to get away from here.

Pause.

It ain't what happened. It's more after Steve.

Darren I can't believe you never even got his body back.

Pause.

Never mind, the Argies, they'll fuckin pay for it now, Doink. Now they've got the Marines an Paras landed an that. (*to Doink*) It's only a matter of time now, mate.

Pause.

Jock My dad reckons they treat everyone like shit, the MOD, the Navy . . .

Doink No they don't.

Darren They ain't been shit with us, Jock.

Pause.

They done pretty well keepin it quiet. You'd think in a place this size someone would have found out.

Doink Yeah. They put us all straight with the story.

Darren And we stuck with it.

Pause.

Jock We still done it.

Doink And?

Jock We still done it.

Pause.

Doink Me mum says she don't care. Says fuck them.

Pause.

Jock You alright, Darren?

Darren Yeah. Why shouldn't I be?

Jock You ain't bothered about the bloke?

Pause.

Darren Makes sense, dunnit? I'm only fifteen so they can't really do nothin with me. If it had been one of you, you'd have got done.

Doink Yeah.

Pause.

Darren (*he picks up Doink's new speargun*) You got this back at least?

Doink Yeah.

Darren Reckon I'll have to make do with that gaff for a while.

Doink Your mum ain't ever gonna let you get a speargun now.

Pause.

Darren (*indicating the speargun*) When they give you it?

Doink Yesterday, mate.

Darren Thank fuck.

Doink Yeah.

Darren It'd be a right fuckin waste if they'd kept it an you never got the chance to use it.

Doink Yeah.

Darren Is it the same spear?

Doink Yeah.

Darren So it has been used, then.

Darren and Doink laugh.

Jock Come on.

Darren What?

93

Pause.

Doink Silly spic shouldn't have been scuba-divin at night. He wouldn't have drowned otherwise.

Doink looks away from Darren. Darren has to look away too. They are suppressing giggles.

Jock It ain't fuckin funny.

They laugh.

Darren Oh come on. It is a bit funny.

They continue laughing. Darren pretends to drown. Jock begins laughing too. Darren picks up Doink's speargun and pulls the spear out. He holds it on his chest and wriggles about on the ground screaming. Doink and Jock laugh hysterically.

Help. I'm drownin.

Laughter.

I need a lifeguard.

Doink You don't sound much like a spic.

Jock (*laughing*) Stop it.

Darren stops and sits up.

Darren He was a shit swimmer.

Pause.

Come on then, let's get lively.

They begin putting on various items of kit. Doink pulls a diver's knife from his bag.

Doink (*to Darren*) You want this knife.

Pause.

Darren That was Steve's?

Doink Yeah.

Pause.

Darren (*takes the knife*) Cheers.

Doink I'm sorry, mate.

Darren 'S alright.

Doink All that stuff I did. Slaggin you an that.

Darren Don't worry about it.

Doink I didn't mean it.

Darren It's alright.

Doink No it ain't. It ain't alright.

Pause.

I shoulda give you a chance.

Darren You can't think like that, mate.

Pause.

You said that they were comin in here and takin what's ours.

Doink I did, yeah, but . . .

Darren You were right, mate. You were right.

Pause.

I knew it would all blow over.

Pause.

Jock (*to Darren*) It ain't blown over.

Darren You reckon?

Jock Yeah.

Pause.

Darren Fuck them.

Doink Yeah.

Darren I ain't scared any more. (*He begins to strap his knife to his leg.*) I ain't been scared since I done it. (*He puts on his mask and snorkel.*) I fuckin done it. (*He picks up the speargun.*) I can hack it.

> *Darren moves towards the water followed by Doink and Jock.*

If they come back again we'll be ready.

> *Jock jumps into the water.*

Be even stronger the next time. We stick together. We can't be beaten.

> *Doink jumps into the water.*

No fuckin spics in Rosia Bay.

> *Darren jumps into the water.*

> *Blackout.*